BULGARIANS - CIVILIZERS OF THE SLAVS

BOJIDAR DIMITROV

BULGARIANS
CIVILIZERS OF THE SLAVS

Translated from the Bulgarian into English
by Marjorie Hall Pojarlieva

BORINA

CONTENTS

© Bojidar Dimitrov, author, 1993, 1995, 2001
© Antoniy Handjiysky, designer
© Vyara Kandjeva, photographer
© Dimiter Angelov, photographer
© Antoniy Handjiysky, photographer
© BORINA Publishing House, Sofia, Bulgaria

Today Bulgaria takes up the south-east corner of Europe - on the borderline between the Old Continent and Asia. Her southern frontier borders on Turkey and, in fact, forms the frontier of Christian Europe - beyond it stretches the immense sea of Islam.

Given up to Joseph Stalin by Churchill and Roosevelt in Yalta, this small Balkan State (with an area of 111,000 square kilometres and a population of nine million) sank into the Soviet sphere of influence for fifty years and is now unknown to Europe. The average European knew only that Bulgaria was Moscow's most loyal satellite ('happenings' like the ones which took place in Hungary, Poland and Czechia did not take place in Bulgaria), that her powerful military industry was selling weapons all over the azimuth, that it looked as though she had something to do with drug trafficking and with the attempt to assassinate the Pope - things which turned out to be untrue and were only propaganda in the last phase of the cold war. In the end Europe was amazed by the bloodless transition to democracy on the downfall of the communist regimes in East Europe - a phenomenon which was unique, and not only in respect to the stormy Balkan Peninsula. And then, after this, Europe again forgot this small country and people, remembering them only on receiving them into the next European set-up.

Very few people know, however, that it was the Bulgarians who first brought the Slav peoples into the mainstream of European medieval Christian civilization (the basis on which the present-day Europe has been built). The credit due to them for the service they rendered in doing this can be gauged, inasmuch as it is known that all through the Middle Ages, right up to the present day, Slav peoples have occupied two-thirds of the territory of Europe and have formed nearly half of its population.

But how did this happen? Let us go back to the years when a united European state - the Roman Empire - collapsed under the pressure of the human waves arising out of the Great Migration of the Peoples, and on its ruins the new European states sprang up, like mushrooms after rain, through the fourth and fifth centuries AD.

THE SLAVS

The land of origin of this tribe, today occupying an enormous part of the dry land of the earth - from Vladivostok to the Oder and from the north Arctic Ocean to the Adriatic - was in Central Europe. The ancient Greek and Roman authors place them in the plains, forests and fenlands between the Oder, the River Wisla and the Baltic Sea. In the south the Slavs got as far as the river valleys of the Bug and the Dniester, and reached the ridges of the Carpathian Mountains.

In their type of race and in their way of life the Slavs, according to the Roman historian Tacitus, resembled the Germans. They were fair, well-built people, who lived a settled life and who were engaged in primitive agriculture, cattle-breeding, hunting and... armed brigandage. Their social organisation was characterized by the domination of the clan communes, uniting temporarily, but not obligatorily, all for any common undertaking - for instance, an armed attack on the borderlands of the Roman Empire. In this epoch State formations were unknown to the Slavs.

At the end of the fourth century there began their re-settlement in all directions of Europe. We can only guess the reasons for the powerful demographic explosion which resulted in enormous waves of human

beings overflowing into the present-day German, Ukrainian, Russian, Byelorussian, Hungarian, Rumanian, Czech, Croatian, Serbian, Greek and Bulgarian lands.

In a short time the Slavs conquered and made settlements all over Europe up to the Elbe in the West, to the Urals and the Volga in the East, and to the Danube in the South. Even today historians still wonder at their irresistible forward drive. Probably their conquests took place at the price of many victims in their ranks - the Slavs had no cavalry, did not possess any armour or other means of defence, and their weapons were very primitive.

To the south of the Danube, the Slav infantry detachments began to appear in the decades round about the end of the fourth and the beginning of the fifth century, Here things seemed to be lost for them -

Batla, an Old Slavonic name for the marshland near the town of Balchik, which has come down to the present day. The area has now been proclaimed a reserve

Kastramartis Fortress which used to defend one of the most westernly passes of the Balkan Range in the period of the Slav attacks in the 6th and 7th c.c.

Slav ceramics

to the south of the Danube there were flourishing areas of the Eastern Roman Empire (Byzantium), thickly populated, with thousands of well-built fortresses connected by roads, and with garrisons armed to the teeth. In spite of this, the incredible happened - in about only one hundred years, in spite of the terrible casualties inflicted by the armies and garrisons of the Romans, the Slavs succeeded in gnawing away all the lines of defence of their opponents and in occupying the whole Balkan Peninsula. From Trieste to Varna and from the Danube to the Peloponnisos. Even to the Peloponnisos, even there, in the same way as Slav tribes settled in the whole of Hellas. The splendid civilization of the Roman Empire collapsed for ever and irrevocably. Enormous Roman cities became derelict

and deserted, churches, amphitheatres, baths, roads and villas were overgrown with brushwood and thorn. In their places there sprang up the numberless straw huts and underground dwellings of the fair-haired new settlers. At the end of the fifth century, like lonely islands in the Slav sea, only Constantinople and Thessaloniki were left. They were still dominated by Eastern Rome and were besieged and terrorized every ten or fifteen years by the notorious Slav incursions, which were so vividly described by the Church writers in the Passionals of countless martyrs.

Just as they had not done anywhere, either in the original homeland or the newly occupied territories, the Slavs did not build up their own State on the Balkan Peninsula. The powerful tribal striving after independence destroyed in the embryo every idea of building

Shoumen Fortress, built in the Middle Ages

Lyutitsa, the Slavonic name of this fortress in the Rhodopes, has come down to the present day

Slav armour and folk-style ceramics

up a State. Everywhere in the Slav world the States would be established centuries later by foreign tribes that were very different in their languages, way of life and race from the Slavs. In Czechia the State would be established by a Frankish merchant, called Saamo, in Poland by Germans, in Russia by Varyags.

In the lands to the south of the Danube this would be done by

THE BULGARIANS

Even up to the present day these people have remained an incredible puzzle for the historians. And it is their early history that is the most puzzling. When they came into touch with Europe they naturally came to the notice of Greek and Latin authors who began to give information about them.

It is considered that the ancestors of the Bulgarians had set out for Europe from the plains along the northern frontier of China in the first century BC. Some contemporary historians even think that the Great Chinese Wall was built to hold back their stormy raids on Chinese lands. Part of their tribe settled on their way to the West, first of all in Western Siberia and then in the Altai Mountains, extending the frontiers of their State formations right to India. In the third and fourth centuries they had already settled in Europe - in the present-day south Russian plains, the Caucasus and Armenia, coming into contact with Persia and Byzantium. Their State formation, called by ancient authors: 'Great Bulgaria' survived in these lands till 630-640 AD.

The way of life and the culture of the Old Bulgarians amaze even present-day historians. Their achievements in all spheres of human knowledge made them

A victorious Bulgarian warrior, shown in relief on a gold jug. 9th c.

Bronze amulet on which a horseman is depicted. 8th or 9th c.

different from the other peoples taking part in the Great Migration. Unlike the barbarians of the steppes - nomads, Yahuns, Avars, Hazars - and also unlike the Slavs, Goths and Vandals who led a settled life but who had a very primitive rural culture, the Bulgarians, whenever they settled anywhere, built enormous cities of stone, which had all the characteristics of a highly developed urban culture - orderly systems of roads and streets, water supply systems, drainage, baths and even heating installations (the so-called hypocausts). Their calendar, a proof of their very exact astronomical and mathematical knowledge, was, and still is today, the most accurate. Twenty years ago the question was raised in the UNESCO by non-Bulgarian scientists whether this calendar should be proclaimed the current one for the whole world. That was because

Pliska, the eastern gate to the first Bulgarian capital

it is really the most accurate one. Analyses of seeds of cereals, found in archeological excavations, have shown that they were high-yielding sorts, such as are obtained after a hundred years' selection work. From bone material unearthed in digs, it has become clear that all the Old Bulgarian medicos performed difficult operations, ones which would be intricate and hard even for a present-day medical surgeon - for instance, trepanation of the skull. The achievements of the Bulgarians in ore output, metallurgy and metal working impress us as being amazing for that time. The great amount of iron extracted made it possible for them to think up and make the instruments and tools they needed and to maintain a fighting force of 30,000 warriors and horses, clad from head to foot in iron. In battles against all the armies of the epoch - against

Pliska, the ruins of the Great Palace

A ceramic vessel made with a hand potter's wheel. Pliska, 8th or 9th c.

those of the barbarian peoples and against those of the civilized Romans - this 'iron wall' had the same effect, for instance, as could be achieved today by an army of tanks attacking infantry companies armed only with light rifles. That is why the Bulgarians were practically invincible - a miracle would have had to happen in order that their army should lose a big battle. That permitted them to save themselves from the ups-and-downs of fortune in this stormy epoch and to be sought for as allies by all the ambitious persons of the period. Very few people know that the striking power of the armies of Attila was, in fact, the Bulgarians. Moreover, the moderation of their wishes makes the political thought of their leaders surprising. With such a powerful military force concen-

trated in their hands, the temptation would be really great to take decisions to become, for instance, masters of the world, as Attila, Tambourlaine, Chingis Han, Justinian and many others made up their minds to do. Considering the actions of the Bulgarian politicians in that epoch, one cannot help coming to the conclusion that their main care was to ensure peace and quiet for their people, avoiding as far as possible risky military undertakings, either for glory or for foreign lands. But in cases of violation of anything Bulgarian the counter action was usually terrible and merciless, the human potential of the enemy was entirely destroyed and their country brought to ruin. Probably this was also done consciously, in order that the danger of fresh violation should be removed, if not for ever, at least for a long time.

Bulgarian society at this time was built up according to a simplified and efficacious pattern. Every member of society was personally free and chose his profession and occupation himself. The religious tolerance was incredible for that epoch - among the Bulgarians there were Animists, Christians, Buddhists, Judaists and Moslems. The State authories were not interested in the faith of their subjects but required strict observance of the civil laws and mainly, of course, loyalty to the State authorities themselves. The highest State authority was in the hands of the Khan, called in the Christian epoch the King. The decisions, however, were not taken authoritarianly but after discussions and voting by the council of the regional administrative governors. Decisions of high State importance were taken by the Council of the People, that

The Balkan Range - the natural fortress of the Bulgarians

is by Parliament, consisting of deputies. It is unfortunately not known how these people had become deputies - was it by direct election or or just by gathering together the most outstanding and respected persons in every sphere of life?

Nothing definite can be said about the type of race to which the Bulgarians belonged and this is not by chance. An incredibly tolerant system of organization of society, open to the individual, attracted people to the Bulgarian lands, wherever these lands happened to be in different chronological periods - attracted people who felt inhibited and restricted in their native communities because of religious, ethnical or class intolerance. It is interesting to note that the name 'Bulgar' itself means 'mixture' and probably was given to them

Deutashlari, proto-Bulgarian tombstones near Pliska, dating to the 8th and 9th c.c.

The fortress wall of the medieval city of Druster (present town of Silistra), the seat of the Bulgarian Patriarch in the time of King Simeon (893-927) and of King Peter I (927-970)

by their contemporaries, to show that the Bulgarian people were a mixture of different peoples.

And, in fact, in excavations of Old Bulgarian necropoles in which there were burials of people with the same manner of life and culture, proofs have come to light that they were all subjects of the same State, although they were of different races - burials of individuals of all the races living at that time, from the Pacific to the Atlantic - from Mongoloids to Aryans.

One thing is sure - the Bulgarians were unusually tall and strong. When the average height of the European in the Middle Ages was 1.60 metres, the average height of the Bulgarian was 1.75 metres. "Ten of our men cannot overcome one Bulgarian" complained an Arabian geographer of that time.

The explanation given by scientists for their ex-

A medieval fortress near the village of Matochina

The end of a gold belt with an oval semi-transparent stone set in the middle

traordinary height and strength is that they ate very much meat and had very much physical exercise. The Bulgarians had numerous highly productive herds which provided them with food and they did strenuous physical exercises in their spell of military service that was obligatory for every healthy man who was of full age.

If the Bulgarians had anything to be proud of at that time, it was their army. Strict military legislation fixed the rights and obligations of the serviceman. The regular military service lasted one or two years. On demobilization the serviceman went home with two horses and his weapons. As it is today in Switzerland and Israel. But he had no right to use these horses for farmwork, or to let his weapons get into a neglected

state. For using a military horse for his own work or for letting his weapons rust, the penalty was only one thing - death. The same penalty was imposed for neglectful fulfilment of duty in military service, both in peace and wartime.

To make up for this, the state authorities took care of servicemen in a way which has only now in the present day become usual and characteristic of the treatment of the military. Peace treaties were never concluded without a special clause to fix the return of prisoners-of-war and the corpses of the dead from enemy territory. Wars would sometimes continue for years only because the enemy refused to return captured Bulgarian soldiers, even when they were few in number. Servicemen did not receive any pay but the

whole community considered it their duty to be of help to them when necessary. Gradually there sprang up a cult of the army, the defender of the people and the State, and reminiscences of this cult remain even today.

With this resolute and extraordinarily efficient army the Bulgarians survived through all storms in the centuries of the great migrations of the peoples, in spite of their relatively small number. I will recall the fact that at that time peoples much more numerous and more famous in battle disappeared - Huns, Avars, Goths, Vandals... And yet in the middle of the seventh century something happened to the Bulgarians that made them leave the lands of the present-day South Russian steppes in which they had settled 300 years before that.

KHAN ASPARUH - IN SEARCH OF A NEW HOMELAND

In the middle of the seventh century the 'Great Bulgaria' was attacked from the south and the east by a powerful tribal union of Hazars, including the multitudinous Turkic steppe tribes. The wars continued for nearly a decade. The starving steppe soldiers had nothing to lose. The steppes had become barren and infertile from the long years of excessive exploitation and that was why the victims, at the price of whom the Bulgarians again repelled the blow, were numerous and grievous. Perhaps that was why the leaders of the 'Great Bulgaria' decided to look for another place in which to settle. Probably they had reached this conclusion in weighing up and analysing the situation and had become convinced that the plains, which are today the South Russian Plains, were too open and that there were no natural lines of defence. And also that these plains were on the way of all the peoples starting from the depths of Asia to Europe and that if this time Hazars had wanted to cross through Bulgaria, then tomorrow others would want to do so too, and the day after a third tribe would also want to do so, and that the number of victims, who would fall in defending this land, would always be too high.

Proto-Bulgarian tent on which are graphic drawings. Limestone model. 8th or 9th c.

The central part of the Balkan Range

Proto-Bulgarian Khan and the Council of Boyls. Artist Nikolai Pavlovich

A tongue-like prolonged applique, part of a gold belt ornament. 8th c.

That was why the people of that former Bulgaria left their cities and villages in one single day and under the protection of the army moved to the lands round the River Oka, in the upper reaches of the River Volga, far away from the route followed by the peoples and from all serious enemies. Here, undisturbed by anyone, Bulgaria flourished for six centuries. She was destroyed only in the thirteenth century by Mongolian Tartars in the time of the apocalyptic invasions in all directions in Europe and Asia.

Three regional rulers of the western regions of the 'Great Bulgaria' did not submit to the decision to move the State. The ancient Byzantine and Latin chroniclers tell us that all three of them were sons of the then already-deceased last Khan of 'Great Bulgaria', Kubrat.

If this is true, we must assume that the decision of the three had been taken with the majority of the people's council in opposition to the opinion of the ruling dynasty.

The fortunes of the three, each of them with several tens of thousands of adherents, were very different from each other. Obviously their strength was not sufficient to oppose the Hazars and that is why the three set off for the West. The eldest, Altzek, reached Bavaria, putting himself at the service of the Bavarian king. It is unknown why this king gave an order one night for the Bulgarians to be killed while they were sleeping. The survivors withdrew fighting and, crossing over the Alps, they went down into Lombardy, where they were well-received. Gradually they were

assimilated by the Italian people, leaving numerous surnames 'Bulgary' and 'Bulgariny'. The second son of Kubrat, called Kuber, reached the present-day Hungary and there put himself at the disposal of the Khan of the Avar State. Later he brought about an uprising against the Avars, then, having succeeded in withdrawing with the population along the frontiers, he settled in the lands of the present-day Macedonia in accordance with an agreement with Byzantium. And the third son, Asparuh, settled with his several tens of thousands of people in the plain around the delta of the Danube. The Bulgarians continued proudly to call this rather small territory of several thousand square kilometres Bulgaria.

The Danubian Plain - the valley of the River Rousse Lom

THE ESTABLISHMENT
OF THE BULGARIAN STATE

Let us return again to the Balkan Peninsula. It was conquered and settled entirely by Slavs in the same years as the 'Great Bulgaria' broke up. But the Slavs did not succeed in establishing their own State here, one which could have protected their conquests and achievements from outside enemies. Recovering from the severe blows it had suffered, the Eastern Roman Empire (Byzantium) was beginning the slow but successful reconquest of the Peninsula in every moment when it was not engaged with the Arabs along its southern frontier. The Byzantine armies were facilitated both by the tribal particularization of the Slavs and by the bad armament of their military forces. Although brave and courageous, the Slavs fought without any defensive armour (naked down to the waist or with linen shirts), only with short swords or spears against the mailed Roman legions. They had neither cavalry nor navy and that was why they were often surprised by the manoeuvres of the Byzantine armed forces, which would often appear unexpectedly in the rear. The low life-style culture was the reason for the low level of their military culture - the Slavs did not use the thousands of fortresses, which were almost all in a state of good repair. These fortresses had come to the

Secret underground passages are characteristic elements in the plan of the castle complex in Pliska

Slavs by inheritance from the Romans when the country had been conquered and they could have been repaired with a small effort, but the Slavs preferred to fight in the forests and swamps. This tactic, which was successful in attack, was hopeless in defence.

Thus Eastern Rome succeeded in the period from 660 to 680 in getting back its control over the lands included in the present-day territories of Greece, Albania, Macedonia, Dalmatia and South Bulgaria. Only the lands of the Roman province of Moesia - the present-day Northern Bulgaria, including the plains between the lower reaches of the Danube and the Balkan Range - remained under the control of the Slav tribes. But here again Byzantium established important bridgeheads, conquering and re-taking all the

Pliska, part of the fortress walls with one of the round towers on it

coastal fortresses with her navy. The important seaport of Varna was one of these fortesses.

In 680 Byzantium prepared her decisive blow which was to restore the old imperial frontier along the Danube. An army, 60,000 strong, was made ready for debarking in Varna in order to break down the opposition of the Slavs from the mouth of the Danube to Belgrade. The mortal danger was felt by the Royal Princes of the seven Slav tribes living in Moesia. Realizing how poor their military forces were, they turned for help to the Khan of the Bulgarians, Asparuh. The agreement which the Bulgarian ruler would impose was hard and uncompromising. There would be help for the Slav territories and the population in the Bulgarian State, but there would have to be recognition of the supreme power of the Bulgarian ruler, and

submission to the Bulgarian laws by the Slavs in Moesia. Of the two evils, both of which would do away with their independence, the Slavs chose the Bulgarian one - they had the promise that the Slav aristocracy would be included in the State administrative system with adequately important posts in the hierarchy.

In her turn Byzantium felt the danger and, instead of the Byzantine navy disembarking 60,000 soldiers, under the personal command of the Emperor Constantine the Fourth Pogonat, in Varna, it landed them at the mouth of the Danube. But this army did not present any problems for Asparuh's extremely highly qualified fighting forces. The regiments of the Bulgarians concealed themselves in the central fortress and the Byzantine army, which was besieging them, be-

King Simeon defeats the Byzantine army near Acheloi, 20.03.917 - a miniature in the Madrid manuscript of Joan Scilitsa

Great Preslav - the second Bulgarian capital

came exhausted with hunger, with sudden strong attacks made by the Bulgarians and with illness. And after a few weeks they emerged from the fortress and drew up in line for the decisive battle. There was no battle in the real sense of the word. At the sight of the famous Bulgarian armoured cavalry lined up in the centre of the battle formation, the Byzantine forces threw away their weapons and rushed back to their ships anchored on the seacoast. At the beginning even the Bulgarians could hardly believe that this was really the psychological breakdown of the enemy and thought that it was a matter of some military trick but, after that, they set about the pursuit of the enemy and destroyed almost the whole of the Byzantine army. The only people who saved themselves were the Emperor and his suite who left the battle formation of the army first of all and escaped with five ships. After the victory Khan Asparuh with a great part of his people and his army occupied the territory of the ancient Roman province of Moesia, which stretched from Belgrade to the mouth of the Danube and which was proclaimed the territory of the State of Bulgaria. In 681 a peace treaty was concluded between Byzantium and Bulgaria and this treaty fixed their frontiers along the ridges of the Balkan Range.

The present-day Bulgarians consider this date to be the birthday of their State. Strictly speaking and from the juridical point of view this is not right. As we have seen the birthday of Bulgaria should be considered to be at least several centuries earlier.

Perhaps for the present-day European of more

The medieval Mezek Fortress

Khan Krum before the walls of Constantinople. Artist Nikolai Pavlovich

interest is the fact that of all the States of the European continent which existed round about 681, only Bulgaria has come through to the present-day with the name which she was born with.

Very important for the further understanding of those times is also the fact that this was the first Slav State. No matter that its ruler and people, some of whom had played a decisive role in its establishment, were of non-Slav origin, the enormous mass of its population were Slavs. There was soon to be an extension of the Bulgarian State, which in a period of only 150 years would take in the territories of the whole of the Balkan Peninsula (except for the southern part of the present-day Greece) and also Wallachia, Moldavia

and Hungary by absorbing many lands in which Slavs had settled. And there was a paradox - the State and population would be known by the non-Slav words 'Bulgaria' and 'Bulgarians'.

In those times there were such paradoxes also in other places in Europe. Russia was established as a State on absolutely the same model by the Varangians around Kiev, who had nothing in common with the Slavs and who had come from Sweden and were called Russians. Do not France and the French whose Gallic-Romanic origin is unquestionable bear the name of the German tribe of Franks.

A medallion showing an animal, probably a lion. It was discovered in Tsarevets in Veliko Turnovo

The fortress walls of Nessebur

BULGARIAN STATE - THE GUARDIAN OF EUROPE IN THE EARLY MIDDLE AGES

The appearence of Bulgaria, a stable, civilized, and strong military power in the European East, had an incredibly favourable effect on European civilization. Even if it were only because her armies stopped the barbarian waves, surging up and periodically pouring from Asia over Western Europe and bringing ruin in their trail, both for the population and the economy. The barbarians had simply nowhere to pass through except through Bulgarian territory. And there they quickly understood at their own cost that the Bulgarians were excellent warriors. Bulgaria also stopped the barbarian attacks on European civilization and Byzantium could already turn to the south and defend itself from the Arabs. It is true that Bulgaria and Byzantium would often have problems but they concerned only the territorial possessions in the Balkans populated by Slavs. Bulgarian political thought never had as its aim the entire destruction of Byzantium or the annexation of areas populated by non-Slav peoples. Moreover the brief military clashes used to alternate with thirty or forty years', or even half a century, periods of peace. This allowed Byzantium, the heir to

The Madara Horseman

The wreath-like rock out of which the Madara Horseman is hewn

ancient European civilization, to survive for another eight centuries, to preserve the achievements of the ancient cultural and technological heritage and to hand them on to Europe, in many cases again through the intermediary called Bulgaria.

We will remind Europeans who know that the Old Continent was saved in the eighth century from the first Islamic aggression at the Battle of Poitiers in 732 AD by the armies of Charles Martel, that the Arab invasion in this epoch proceeded simultaneously through the two entrances to Europe - the Straits of Gibraltar and the Bosphorus. And that, although the Arabs got through the Straits of Gibraltar and conquered the Iberian Peninsula and held it for a long time, striving to continue in their drive into Europe before being stopped by Charles Martel, on the

The medieval Fortress of Pernik

Bosphorus they were mercilessly defeated by the Bulgarians, thrown out of Europe and beaten back deep into Asia and, moreever, for a rather long period, in spite of the fact that in this part of Europe the Arabs had attacked with much greater forces than they had done through Gibraltar.

The events are well worth describing - many Arab, Greek, Latin and Old Bulgarian authors, contemporaries of the battles, have left accounts of the events. Overwhelming the Byzantine armies in Asia Minor, an Arab army of 100,000 crossed into Europe and besieged the capital Constantinople in 717. The city was besieged, its supplies were running out, hunger loomed up and it looked as though it would fall.

Suddenly a Bulgarian army appeared on the hills in

front of the Arabs' camp. In the first moment the people of Constantinople were confused and upset - they had not looked for help from the Bulgarians, because several years before this they had been waging war with them for a Slav region. They thought that the Bulgarians would take advantage of their difficult situation and ally themselves with the Arabs in order to put an end to thc Empirc. But after the Bulgarians had slaughtered several detachments of Arabs going around outside their camps - slaughtered them in sight of the besieged people of Constantinople - they were reassured and convinced that an unexpected ally had arrived.

Bulgaria's intervention had obviously not been sparked off by the wish for territorial expansion - after the events the Bulgarians withdrew without claiming

Silver-plated chain-armour, 10th c.

any compensation. Their opposition to the Arabs was obviously due to an ever-growing consciousness of belonging to one community - the community of the European Christian civilization - the values of which were threatened by a powerful enemy who had nothing in common with this civilization. Although Christianity was still not the official religion in Bulgaria, it was professed by a large part of the population and by the Bulgarian ruler Khan Terval himself. That was why that in this case the lasting hostility between Byzantium and Bulgaria was quickly forgotten in the name of their common survival.

The Arab forces, although they found themselves between two terrible dangers (the Constantinople garrison and the Bulgarian army), were considerably

Bulgarian warriors in the Menology of the Emperor Basil II. 11th c.

Column on which there are Bulgarian words in Greek letters, announcing a peace treaty concluded between the Bulgarians and Byzantines

more numerous than those of the two allies taken together. However their military commanders decided not to start a great battle with the Bulgarians. Although excellent cavalrymen, the Arabs had no armoured cavalry fighters. That is why they shut themselves up in their camp, which surrounded Constantinople on all sides, and continued the siege.

But the things were already changing. Recovering from the first shock, the Byzantine fleet stole out of the Bosphorus and dealt a smashing blow at the Arab fleet. In this way it ensured the conveyance of food to Constantinople and stopped, at least at sea, the provisioning of the Arab camp. The Bulgarians took care of stopping it on land - the Arab supply detachments were killed by the Bulgarian light cavalry, mostly at only a mile from their camp. Now hunger also loomed up in the Arab camp. Yet the Arabs held out a whole year. Only in the summer of 718 their army stole out of its camp and got into battle formation against the Bulgarians. This was obviously an act of desperation, the Arab generals knew that they had no chance against the armoured Bulgarian cavalry, which had been stationed for a whole year in a state of tedium and inaction on the hills of Constantinople. And actually the Arab cavalry, which first sallied forth to attack, was crushed literally in a few minutes by the mailed horses and fighters of the Bulgarians. The Frankish authors give different figures for the casualties of the Arabs killed by the Bulgarians. Sigebert wrote that the Bulgarians killed 30,000 Saracens, the monk Alberic figures the Arab casualties out at 32,000. The number of the dead was not so important in this case - the most important thing was that it was all over with the Arab siege. The Arabs were not only thrown out of Europe but also pursued and hounded by the Bulgarian-Byzantine detachments in Asia Minor, and pushed back to the frontiers that Byzantium had had before the conflict. This meant that a Christian barrier was built up against Islam, a barrier which would last for the whole of seven centuries more. It was only in the fourteenth and fifteenth centuries that Islam made a second attack, which was led this time by the Ottoman Turks and which ended up with the defeat of Bulgaria and Byzantium. These two had failed to unite as they had united in the eighth century against the common enemy. And the lack of support for the Christian East by the West of Europe in the fourteenth century finally brought Islam right up to the walls of Vienna, Venice and Warsaw. But this is connected with another theme.

Medieval Nessebur

Ꙗ priumpo Regi trume

BULGARIA AND EUROPE FROM THE EIGHTH THROUGH THE TENTH CENTURY

The appearance of the first Slav State in Europe and the development of its power inevitably turned it into a centre uniting the Slavs in South-East and Central Europe. Bulgaria had a specially strong power of attraction for those Slav tribes that had lost their independence and were included within the frontiers of the non-Slav State formations - the Eastern and

The feast of Khan Krum after his victory over the Emperor Nicophorus - miniature in the Manasses Chronicle. 14th c.

Western Roman Empires, the Avar Haganat...

In the seventh and ninth centuries, cases of separating areas populated by Slavs in these State formations and uniting these areas with Bulgaria were frequent occurrences. As a result of this, Bulgaria's territory was gradually extended and by the middle of the ninth century it had already become an enormous Slav Empire, the frontiers of which stretched from the present-day eastern borderline of Austria to the River Don and from the surroundings of Krakow in Poland to the coast of the Aegean Sea.

Ensuring peace and quiet for Western Europe by stopping the barbarian invasions, Bulgaria was able to have her say also in respect to the principal question concerting the fate of the Old Continent in this epoch,

Death of the Bulgarian King Peter and the return of his sons from Constantinople to Preslav - miniature in the Manasses Chronicle

namely the way of its development.

The possibilities were two. One was the establishment of a unified European State - this meant in practice to restore the Roman Empire. The ideological basis, on which this superstate would have rested, was, of course, Christianity, and the language of the population would have been Latin or Greek. The arguments in favour of this political idea came again from Christianity: "One God in Heaven, One Kingdom of Heaven", that its projection on Earth should be the same "One kingdom, one religion, one people and one language". To realize this idea it would have been necessary to destroy all the national States which variegated the map of Europe with their frontiers after the final downfall of the Roman Empire in 476, and also to dissolve all the new and old European nations in the cauldron of one projected Latin or Greek nation. This conception of the uniting of Europe, however, had nothing in common with the present-day one of a United Europe - a Europe of united nations and cultures.

The other possibility was to keep the right to independent existence and development of each European nation - the way along which Europe set out in the end. The greatest credit for this must go to the Bulgarian political thought of that time and its realization on the European political scene.

At the end of the eighth century and in the first half of the ninth century, when the question of the choice of the way for the political and cultural development of Europe was being solved, the things seemed to have been decided beforehand in favour of the universalistic

A small bronze statue - a key from Pliska. 9th or 10th c.

Krivus Fortress in the valley of the River Arda

conceptrion, because of the fact that the principal theological and political forces in Europe were backing it up and acting to further it.

In the West these were the Roman Empire (the Frankish Empire) and the Papacy. In the East they were the Eastern Roman Empire (Byzantium) and the Oecumencial Patriarch of Constantinople.

Actually they have been called Western or Frankish and Eastern or Byzantine by the historians to facilitate their scholarly reasearches. The political leaderships of the two European Great Powers called them both the Roman Empire and their subjects Romans - a clear sign of their claims to the political, historical and cultural heritage. The Patriarch of Constantinople and the Pope of Rome stood firmly behind the claims respectively of Eastern and Western Rome.

In the political pattern of Eastern Europe the universal idea was uphelp by the powerful Byzantium - her possessions were still stretched out over large territories in Asia, the Balkan Peninsula and Italy. In the West the Emperors of the Holy Roman (the Frankish) Kingdom gave their steady backing to this idea, too.

Towards the end of the eight century the universal idea began to acquire concrete content. In the East, Byzantium recovered all the former provinces of the Roman Empire which had been occupied in previous centuries by Slavs, with the exception of Moesia, a part of the Bulgarian State. In the West, with fire and sword, the Emperor Charlemagne (768-814) united the whole of Western Europe from its frontiers with the Arabs, along the ridges of the Pyrenees to the middle

A vessel from the gold treasure found in Nagyszent-miklos. 9th c.

A gold medallion that belonged to Khan Omourtag. 9th c.

The Byzantine Emperor Joan Tsimishi setting out against Preslav in 971 - a miniature in the Manasses Chronicle

reaches of the Danube. In reality towards the end of the eighth century there were three States in Europe: two of them claiming to be the heirs 'de jure' to the Roman Empire and the State built up on a national basis, Bulgaria. For Bulgaria it was very fortunate that, although they were not waging war against each other, the first two pretenders to the Roman heritage were irreconcilable enemies. But in 800 this favourable circumstance seemed about to disappear. The ambassadors of the two pretenders to Rome succeeded in negotiating a dynastic marriage beween the Empress Irene, ruling Eastern Rome at that time, and Charlemagne. The realization of this marriage would have led automatically to uniting the two parts of the Roman Empire and, in reality, to its complete restoration, with the exception of two provinces - Moesia and Dacia which formed the territory of Bulgaria. It is not difficult to guess what would have been the fate of Bulgaria, in spite of her powerful army, if she had been faced with the military resources of the whole of Europe and no small part of Asia. She would have been literally crushed in a few weeks and, moreover, on a legitimate basis, because she was then occupying a part of the Roman heritage.

But one of the ensuing plots, hatched around the Bosphorus, dethroned the Empress Irene and put a man in her place. Thus the effort to unite the two parts of the Empire by way of a dynastic marriage, at least up to then, was marked by failure. In spite of this, hard times set in for Bulgaria. The new Emperor of Byzantium, the ambitious and gifted Nicephore I

Logothete, decided to destroy Bulgaria and undertook a number of campaigns against her. The failures in the first years did not make him waver - in counter offensives in 809 the Bulgarians took Sofia for ever (this city is their present-day capital). Then, after this, they conquered the chief Byzantine fortresses in the Balkans, but the paralysing Byzantine military actions continued with disheartening regularity.

The campaign in 811 was particularly crucial. A Byzantine army of eight thousand men, gathered from all regions of the Empire, crushed several Bulgarian corps and even took the Bulgarian capital of Pliska. In a great battle, however, on July 26, 811 the Bulgarian army, in which young women had also been mobilized and which was commanded by Khan Krum, encircled

Gold medallion from Preslav. 10th c.

The Emperor Nicephore attacking Bulgaria and his capture by the Bulgarians - a miniature in the Manasses Chronicle. 14th c.

Khan Krum's warriors pursuing and wounding the son and heir of Nicephore - Stavracius, a miniature in the Manasses Chronicle

King Peter's lead seal

and wiped out the Byzantine forces to the last man. The Emperor Nicephore I Logothete was also killed. His skull, plated with gold, was made into a goblet from which Khan Krum used to drink at the time of the Bulgarians court ceremonies. The counter offensive of the Bulgarians led to fresh grim but victorious battles for the Bulgarians in the South Balkan provinces of Byzantium. The last decisive battle was at Versinikiya in March 813. The 30,000 armoured Bulgarian cavalry were the decisive factor in bringing victory to the Bulgarians. In the summer of 813 Bulgarian forces were already under the walls of Constantinople. True to their usual prudence, the Bulgarians did not try to destroy Byzantium entirely by taking the capital - something which could have been done very easily now that the Byzantine army had been totally destoyed at Versinikiya. This, however, would have made them neighbours of the Moslem Arab East and would have brought them face to face with new problems. Khan Krum contented himself with driving only his spear into the fortress wall of Constantinople as a sign of victory, and went back to Bulgaria. Then peace negotiations were begun and these ended with uniting the most fruitful Eastern Roman province, Thrace, with Bulgaria. Drained of her resources in men and exhausted, Byzantium was no longer a military threat to Bulgaria.

Now her military machine could turn quietly to the threat from the West. For about two decades the ambitions of Charlemagne in respect to the Bulgarian lands could hardly be restrained by Bulgarian diplomacy, trying with great efforts to prevent war on two fronts. Objectivity requires that we should say that if Charlemagne had not been so baleful towards Constantinople and had not decided to observe the downfall of his rival for the Roman throne with gloating, Bulgaria would hardly have been able to survive. And Europe would have set out along another way.

So the Bulgarian armies moved along the frontiers of the States in Central Europe. Again true to their usual prudence, the Bulgarians proposed that the disputable questions concerning the frontiers, ones which might provoke war, should be settled by negotiations. In 824 in Aachen, according to the chronicler Einhardt, the biographer of Charlemagne, and according to the annals of the Fulda Monastery, a Bulgarian mission arrived and wished to get the question of the

The Bulgarians defeating the Byzantine army near Bulgarophigon in 896 - miniature in the Madrid manuscript of Joan Scilitsa

"frontiers and borders between the Franks and Bulgarians" settled. The heir to Charlemagne, the Emperor Louis the Pious, in spite of the insistence of the Bulgarian mission, prolonged the negotiations for the whole of three years. It became clear to the Bulgarians that the Holy Roman Empire was not interested in fixing the frontiers between it and Bulgaria because of its claims to the Roman heritage, which included the whole of Bulgaria.

This time the Bulgarian political establishment, which was guiding the country and at the head of which was Khan Omurtag, the son of the victor over Byzantium, Khan Krum, decided not to engage in any experiments to prove the ability of the Bulgarian army to repel any blow dealt at the country, but to attack

King Simeon's envoys giving his message to the Emperor Lev VI, the Philosopher - miniature in the Madrid manuscript of the Chronicle of Joan Scilitsa

first. In 827 the Bulgarian Danubian fleet sailed up the Rivers Drava and Tissa and penetrated deep into the territory of the Franks, landing forces at a number of places and taking large stretches of territory populated by Slavs. The war continued for two years and, in spite of the efforts of Louis the Pious who sent even his son Louis the German against the Bulgarians, the forces of the Holy Roman Empire lost battle after battle. A peace treaty was concluded in 829 and, according to it, one more Roman province (Panonia, in the present-day Hungary) was added to the territory of Bulgaria. This conflict is interesting also because in its vicissitudes one future big European capital, Budapest, was born. It arose out of two Bulgarian military frontier fortresses, Buda and Pest, situated on the two

banks of the Danube. By the mid-ninth century the Bulgarians had succeeded in taking one more of Byzantium's big provinces. This was Macedonia, famous both in Antiquity and in more recent times. Moreover this breakaway from Byzantium and union with Bulgaria took place in 837 in a peaceful way, after the leading Macedonians had turned with a request to the Bulgarian ruler to accept them into his State. Byzantium had no power to oppose them. Moreover, the Bulgarians helped Byzantium to survive again in 822, crushing the revolt of a renegade who, backed up by an Arab army, besieged Constantinople.

King Simeon's lead seal

The victory of Bulgaria in the dramatic conflicts with the two heiresses to Rome in the first half of the ninth century led to the survival of an enormous part of the Slavs in Southern, Central and Eastern Europe, who were saved in this way from assimilation and were united within the framework of one State. The States defeated in the wars with Bulgaria - States which were the bearers and fulfillers of the universal idea in respect to the future of Europe - were left without military power in the epoch when the only way to realize this idea was by means of military power. On the European political scene, besides the two 'Roman' colossals, a third superpower had appeared - the national State of Bulgaria. Skilfully balancing between the two giants, Bulgaria did not let further attempts to restore Rome and to realize the Roman idea have any success at all. The breakup of the Frankish Empire and birth of the new European States, already on a national basis, took place not only on the Bulgarian model, but also often through the direct protection (most of all in South-Eastern Europe) of the then powerful Bulgarian Kingdom. The contradictions between the three superpowers, built up on different ideological bases, actually helped the new States to live more easily through the juvenile period of their history.

A gold jug from the Nagyszentmiklos treasure. 9th c.

THE EVANGELIZATION OF BULGARIA

In 852 Khan Boris I ascended the throne. After several insignificant clashes at the beginning of his reign with the Eastern Roman Empire and German Kingdom (obviously the Great Powers of that epoch were sounding the young ruler), Boris I ruled for nearly half a century in peace with all his old and new neighbours. The brilliant diplomacy of Boris I settled

King Boris with a cross in his hand and a crown on his head - miniature in the teacher's Tetraevangelia of Constantine of Preslav
The Cross over the throne. 1601

all the disputed foreign-policy questions by negotiations, finishing with peaceful treaties, above all treaties of alliance. Towards the middle of his reign the situation was somewhat paradoxical. Bulgaria was in military and political alliance with the States in the whole of Central and Eastern Europe, but these were frequently irreconcilable enemies in respect to each other.

In fact the peaceableness of the Bulgarian ruler was also due to the fact that, already in the time of his predecessors, the natural frontiers of the Bulgarian State had been reached. All the Slavs in South-Eastern Europe had been united within the frontiers of Bulgaria. This land had been separated from the West Slavs (Poland and Czechia) and from the East Slavs (Russia) by territories populated by non-Slav people - Avars, Magyars, Patchanags and Kumans. True to the well-known Bulgarian moderation, Boris I did not get himself involved in exhausting wars with these steppe peoples. Moreover, in the lands of the Western and Eastern Slavs there began to appear the first State formations and Boris I could not hope for a natural Slav gravitation towards Bulgaria. She was already not the only Slav State.

'The profound peace' (as it was called by the East Roman writers) allowed Boris I and his political entourage to pay attention to a serious internal problem. Anticipating the events, we will say that his decision would turn Bulgaria into the civilizing centre of the Slav people and States.

The Old Metropolitan Bishop's Church in Nessebur, dating to the second half of the 5th c.

It was a matter of choosing to have one religion only, one which would be proclaimed the State religion, and of doing away with the incredible tolerance in respect to religious matters, a tolerance which was almost beyond belief for a medieval State of Europe at that time and which we have already mentioned. This tolerance had begun to give rise to problems. Although Bulgaria was one national State, the Bulgarian people were divided up into almost a dozen religious communities.

Part of the people populating the Bulgarian lands were still pagans. Some of them believed in the god Tangra, who had been worshipped by the Bulgarians while they were still living at the foot of the Himalayas. The pagans of Slav origin believed in about twenty gods at least - Perun, Lada, Volos - the Slav soul and

imagination were really prolific. There were others who were Buddhists or Moslems. The Christians were, however, in the majority, especially after uniting with the provinces of Thrace and Macedonia which had been entirely converted to Christianity by Byzantium. But the Christians were not all unanimous - in her heritage Bulgaria received, along with the Christians in Thrace and Macedonia, all the possible heresies of Byzantine Orthodoxy - Paulicians, Manichaens, Arians. "My country is full of preachers of many religions," complained Boris in his letter to Pope Nicolas I.

As is known the religious communities in the Middle Ages were often in conflict with each other, as they sometimes are even today, and this weakened the unity of the country in which they were living. Some-

A fantastic mask, a combination of a human face and the head of an animal, most probably that of a lion, from a mural in the church of the Nedelishky Monastery. The depiction of a mask on either side of the oltar was a violation of church canon law and this mask is something unique in Bulgarian ecclesiastical art. It is probably a remainder of very old pagan traditions.

Three crosses from Pliska, 9th or 10th c. The first two crosses are gold, the third is of wood. They are placed so as to form a triple cross. Christian scenes are depicted on them in chronological order

times conflicts arose even among Christians of one and the same denomination. One hagiographer of this same epoch described the lives of the martyrs of Tiveriopol - a passional which, in some passages, verges on the tragi-comic. In the pandemonium of waging war against Byzantium, the citizens of a Christian city in Macedonia stole relics from another neighbouring Christian city and laid them in their Cathedral Church. When the war was over the citizens of the city from which the relics had been stolen wanted to have them back again, but the other city would not return them. The negotiations of the two Christian communities finished without having any results and the people of the two cities, armed with whatever they could lay their hands on, were ready for battle - one side trying to keep the relics and the other side trying to get them back. The regional governor, who was a pagan, a worshipper of Tangra, and who had not any idea how Christian problems could be solved, was in a quandary. Finally he became angry and solved the problem like a soldier - he brought heavily armed soldiers into the two cities to keep the citizens from killing each other, and he divided the relics into two equal parts and each city received one-half.

There was another thing which troubled Boris I and, from the point of view of the State, it was far more serious. Religious pluralism did not allow common legislation to be introduced for all subjects of the State in all spheres of life. Let us take as an example family laws and property laws. According to the laws of their

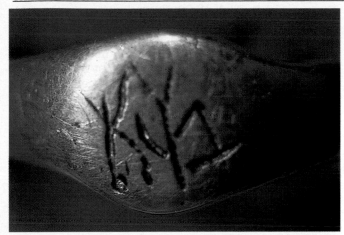

religion, the Animists had the right to two wives and the Moslems to four, while in some Christian sects women and children were held in common. We can imagine what a muddle it was when it was a question of determining property and heritage rights.

A gold ring on which runes are inscribed from the city of Rila. 9th c.

It was necessary to put an end to religious tolerance. Of the numerous possibilities he had in making his choice of an official State religion, Boris I chose Christianity. Much has been written about the motives underlying his choice. The medieval Byzantine and Latin authors, filled with enthusiasm about the conversion of the third European superpower to Christianity, speak about the Divine Light which appeared to Boris in his dream and about the poweful preaching of his sister, a Christian, that convinced him of the truth of the Christian Faith.

And anyway one of his first considerations would be that the predominant part of the population of Bulgaria had already been converted to Christianity. To proclaim to this population that from the next day the Christians would have to worship Mohammed, Tangra or Perun would have meant a revolt and bloodshed and civil war.

And secondly Boris I was unquestionably attracted by the ethical and moral values of Christianity. Garbed in legislative form, a codex of laws, in line with the norms of the Christian faith, had been prepared long before this and enforced in the Christian States in Europe - they undoubtedly led to order in the community and did away with all inconsistencies on a religious or a civil basis.

Thirdly, Boris I considered that Bulgaria was in

Khan Boris I is converted to Christianity. Artist Nikolai Pavlovich

A two-storey church - the burial place of Assenova Fortress

Europe and that all the State formations in the Old Continent were Christian. As a statesman he knew that the power of the sword, with which Bulgaria had awed her neighbours up to then, was not permanent. The wars which had broken out against Bulgaria for purely worldly reasons in the past, because of one stretch of territory or another, had often turned into religious wars - 'wars against the infidel Bulgarians'. And through the medieval centuries there was nothing that inspired the eventual enemy more than a war against 'infidels'. With the acceptance of Christianity Boris I hoped to knock this trump card out of the hands of his potential foreign political opponents. In public opinion the war between Christian States was a 'disgraceful and unworthy' thing. Everything was done to

prevent such a war, but when such a war did break out, it was made considerably more humane. For instance, prisoners-of-war were not killed and people were not captured to be made slaves, but soon after the battles were over they were freed. Because in the holy Christian books it was written that Christians could not take other Christians into captivity or into slavery.

Thus in 863 Boris I was baptized along with the whole of his court and, probably because of political considerations and so as not to offend anyone, he sent for priests to come from Constantinople, the Papacy and the German Kingdom to help convert the non-Christian part of his people. This was completed by the summer of 864. Christianity was proclaimed by a State decree to be the only religion permitted by the State

and the Christian laws - the common laws for all subjects.

Actually these things did not pass without giving rise to some troubles. In some outlying areas, inhabited mainly by pagans, a revolt broke out. The lightly armoured forces of the rebels succeeded in reaching the capital of Pliska and in getting into rank in battle formation in front of it. According to the contemporary Greek and Latin Christian authors, Boris I went out alone and stood in front of the rebels without any weapon, holding only a Holy Cross in his hand. He raised it high up over his head and, thanks to its power, the forces of the rebels ran away and their leaders gave themselves up without fighting. This event was described in scores of dramas, novels and poems by

The conversion of the Royal Preslav court to Christianity

Assenova Fortress

*Rila Monastery founded
in the 10th c.*

*Charter granted to Rila
Monastery by King Ivan
Shishman in 1378. Na-
tional Museum of Rila
Monastery*

Christian authors of Western Europe in the period
from the ninth through the seventeenth century. Whether it was only by the miraculous power of the Holy
Cross or whether it was with the help of his enormous
military power is not clear, but the fact is that Boris I
succeeded in crushing the opposition of the pagans,
and Bulgaria became a Christian State.

The Christianization of Bulgaria gave rise, however, to a foreign political problem. Which of the two
already-formed administrative centres of European
Christianity (Constantinople or Rome) should the Bulgarian dioceses adhere to. The Roman and Greek
priests officiating in Bulgaria were waging an infuriat-
ed war against each other. Boris I himself had a long
and wordy correspondence both with the Pope and the

Constantinople Patriarch. Unquestionably his aim
was to achieve the maximum possible independence of the Bulgarian Church according to ecclesiastical law. After six years' negotiations
Constantinople turned out to be more generous
and offered the Bulgarian Church autocephalism.
But this time too, Boris I showed himself to be a
wise statesman. In order that the choice should
not seem to be his, he proclaimed himself to be
incompetent in respect to Church affairs
and formally stated his wish that the
question should be solved by the
Oecumenical Council. This Council took
place in 870 - it turned out that the Papal
delegates were in the minority, and the
Bulgarian question was raised only at

the very end of the Council, when some Roman delegates had already left. The Bulgarian high-ranking
clergy declared that they were not able to make up
their minds whom to be subordinate to in respect to
their Church administration. Then the Constantinople
delegate asked them: "What Church and priests did
you find when you conquered the lands in which you
live." The answer was: "Greek". That settled the
matter. The Bulgarian Church with the rank of
Archbishopric and comprising seven bishoprics was
subordinate to the Patriarch in Constantinople. But
it was declared to be autocephalous (selfgoverning).
That meant that its subordination was purely for-
mal. Fifty-seven years later it would declare itself to
be a completely self-governing bishopric.

*St John the Baptist's
Church - Nessebur. 14th c.*

Raphide

THE OLD BULGARIAN (SLAVONIC) SCRIPT

Evangelization once again raised a problem. But the Bulgarian statesmen foresaw it, they were aware of it and were prepared to deal with it. As is known, Christianity is a religion which cannot be professed without books and literacy. The Gospels were written down in a book. Every day there was read the 'Life of a Saint' in accordance with the Church calendar, and in this calendar there was one or even dozens of saints for every day of the year. Christianity was sermons, philosophical analyses, interpretations - and all were written down in books. The written Word in the holy Christian books was law - and any divergence or alteration was defined as heresy.

In these centuries the trilingual dogma was in force in the Christian Church. According to it Christianity could be professed in only three languages - Hebrew, Greek and Latin. All Christianity, professed in any other spoken language or written in any other script, was regarded as heresy.

This circumstance could not, of course, arouse enthusiasm in Bulgaria. The Greek language was natural for Byzantium - in this Empire the majority of the people were Greek. Although Latin had been a dead

A depiction of Cyril and Methodius in the menology of Basil II, 11th c. It is in the Library of the Vatican

Asemanievo Evangelium, - an Old Bulgarian Glagolitic manuscript of the 10th c.

language for many years, it was to some degree understandable, at least for the Romanic States in Europe, but all the 'sacred' languages were completely alien to Slavonic. How could God's Word and the wisdom of the Church Fathers reach the ordinary man, if they were professed in the completely ununderstandable Greek and Latin languages? What would have been the estrangement of the intelligentsia from the people, if the former had read and written in Greek or Latin but the latter knew only spoken Slavonic?

And would not Byzantium, the constant rival of Bulgaria in the Balkans, have taken advantage of the fact that the clergy and administration had had Greek educations in order to create their own lobby in Bulgarian religious and State life? With all the dangers this would have involved for the unity of the State.

It was clear what was necessery. A Slavonic alphabet and script had to be created and had to attain canonical recognition by Rome and Constantinople - by the universally known Church leaders of Christianity at that time.

The story of the creation and consolidation of the Slavonic alphabet and script is like a fairy-tale. The amazing thing is that everything in the story is true, because there is confirmation of it in a great number of authentic sources, independent of each other.

The direct creators of the Slavonic alphabet were the two brothers Cyril and Methodius of Thessaloniki, the second largest city in Byzantium. They were the sons of the Governor of the Military-Administrative Region of Thessaloniki, that is they were the children

of one of the highest-ranking aristocrats of the Empire. They themselves affirmed in writing about their own lives that they came from a 'royal family', that means that they were descendants of some Bulgarian ruler. Actually this was possible - in the middle of the eighth century several Bulgarian rulers were dethroned in dynastic struggles and were forced to emigrate to Byzantium. There they enjoyed high aristocratic status and were given administrative posts. The two brothers' excellent knowledge of the Bulgarian language is an argument in favour of this possibility.

In accordance with their rank, the two brothers went to study in the Magnaur School in Constantinople, the one and only university in Europe at that time. On their graduation both of them were given high-ranking administrative posts. The elder one, Methodius, was appointed as Governor of a large military-administrative region Thessalia and Cyril, who had shown from early youth that he had brilliant intellectual qualities, was appointed as the chief librarian in the Patriarchal Library. This post, which seems today to be very modest, was usually held in Byzantium by the future Patriarch of Constantinople.

To the great disappointment of the Emperor and the Patriarch, the two brother suddenly cut short their brilliant careers in 855. They retired to a monastery, boldly declaring that they had decided to dedicate themselves to evangelizing the Slavs and that this would be done more easily when there was a Slavonic script. They rejected the accusation that the new script was of an uncanonical nature with arguments which

An old discus. 10th c.

Cyril and Methodius as depicted in the Radzivilov (Königsberg) Chronicle

Scenes from the lives of SS Cyril and Methodius, a mural in the Arapovski Monastery

were strong enough. "Does not God send the sun and air and rain to all the people?" said Cyril in protest. "That is the proof that God loves all the people in the same way. Why then do you think that God wishes to be glorified in the languages of only three peoples".

The unexpected decision of the brothers Cyril and Methodius coincided strangely with the already declared desire of the Bulgarian King Boris I to be converted to Christianity with the whole of his people. That is why that, in spite of the lack of concrete data on this matter, it can be taken for granted that Boris I had told the two brothers of his misgivings about the practice of Christianity in Bulgaria in the Greek or Latin language, and asked them to help him to overcome his difficulty. Some even see romantic incentives, besides the great love of Cyril and Methodius for the

Slav poeple. According to them, Cyril became known to Boris through Anna, the sister of the Bulgarian King. As is known, she studied with Cyril in the Magnaur School. It was natural and understandable that there should spring up a great love, which motivated Cyril still more in working for the good of the Slavs.

By 862 the two brothers had created the alphabet and translated the fundamental liturgical books into Slavonic languages. Quiet and untroubled now that he had a weapon in his hands, Boris I was converted to Christianity the very next year. Of course, he could not introduce divine service immediately in the Slavonic language - at lightning speed Rome and Constantinople would have declared him a heretic along with all his people. It was necessary to achieve canonical recogni-

A page from the Asemanievo Evangelium - a detail of a capital letter - an Old Bulgarian Glagolitic manuscript of the 10th c.

A miniature of St Matthew, the Evangelist. 14th c.

tion of the Slavonic script and for thousands of clergy and teachers to be trained in advance.

The canonical recognition of the Slavonic alphabet came most unexpectedly, first of all from Constantinople. In the same year, 862, the Moravian Prince Rostislav, who had also been converted to Christianity, turned to the Emperor in Constantinople with a request to send him priests who spoke a Slavonic language (as his people did not understand the Latin sermons of the German priests sent by the Pope). Rostislav promised in return to bring his country into the Byzantine sphere of influence. Constantinople decided that it would not be bad to separate another country from the sphere of Papal influence but, at the same time, the Emperor and the Patriarch realized that if the trilingual dogma were adamantly defended

this would not take place. Moravia was far away. There were not any other means of influencing her and that was why that in Constantinople the Patriarch personally made concessions unheard of up to then in the history of the Church. He blessed the new alphabet and proclaimed it to be fully canonical. On their way to Moravia Cyril and Methodius, of course, went through Bulgaria. Boris I put a group of young people, the sons of Bulgarian nobles, into their charge to study the new script. For seven years Cyril and Methodius preached in the Slavonic language in Moravia, struggling desperatly against the attacks of the Latin clergy. In 869 Pope Nicolas I summoned them to Rome to explain the matter for, after all, they were preaching in a Papal Diocese. It was clear that trouble was brewing, but while they were on their way to Rome, Pope Nicolas I

died. The new Pope Adrian II had some problems concerning his throne - rather many of the influental circles of society in Rome were against his having been chosen as Pope. In searching for an ally, he decided to ask for the help of Byzantium. And he believed that if he supported the work of Cyril and Methodius, whom he considered to be Byzantine agents in the Papal Diocese, he would get the help that he was looking for from Constantinople.

That was why that instead of being insulted, abused and condemned as heretics, Cyril and Methodius were received in Rome as heroes of Christianity with triumphal processions, prayers, etc. - with a special divine service in the Church of Santa Maria Maggiore. The Slavonic alphabet and script were proclaimed to be

A list in the Asemanievo Evangelium - an Old Bulgarian Glagolitic manuscript of the 10th c.

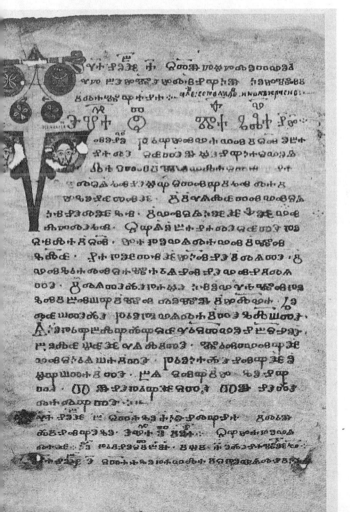

Climent of Ohrid - a mural in the church in the town of Elena

fully canonical, and the Slavonic books were sanctified personally by the Pope. In 879 this act was also endorsed by Pope Johann VIII. Unfortunately the two brother were not able to see Bulgaria again - Cyril died in Rome and several years later Methodius also died. After Methoius' death the German clergy in Moravia forbid the Slavonic alphabet to be used. But the great work had been done and the torch was taken over by Cyril and Methodius' Bulgarian adherents - Clement, Naum, Angelaria, Ghorazd and dozens of others whose names are unknown and who took the management of the Bulgarian Church and culture into their hands when they returned to Bulgaria from Moravia. They introduced the native language in the Church and kept to the decisions of the Eighth Oecumenical Council. They also opened schools in every parish. Training in the native colloquial language proved to be easy and quick. In the West at this time and for centuries later, the dead Latin language was accepted as the literary language, but only those who had dedicated themselves to it were ableto speak and to write Latin. These were the clergy and part of those engaged in politics. According to the estimation of authoritative scholars, no more than two or three per cent of the people were literate. But in Bulgaria literacy, according to the same scholars, took in 65-70 per cent of the people.

SS Cyril and Methodius - an icon

BULGARIA -
THE CENTRE OF SLAVONIC
CHRISTIAN CIVILIZATION

It is well known in Western Europe that the positions of Christianity and literacy were set back after the barbarization of this part of the continent in the period from the third through the fifth century, after and in spite of the unflagging and steadfast work of thousands of Irish monks. These sons of Ireland, descendants of an ancient people, survived in the massacres of the barbarian invasions and then went towards the West with the Gospels in hand, converting newcomers, building churches, restoring old church structures and establishing new ones.

In Eastern Europe this was carried out by the Bulgarians.

Today it is difficult to ascertain whether the motives of the Bulgarian monks, who had spread out in the Slav world from the Oder to the Urals, were dictated by Christian zeal, as they were in the case of the Irish monks. There was really very great zeal evinced in their work, particularly in respect to the newly baptized. In the historical sources there are no data about the State taking part and acting in this. But it is probable that some of these monks were really sent by the Bulgarian State - Christianization and Old

Bookmen in a scriptorium in Preslav

Sacret vessels. 17th c.

Bulgarian literacy naturally created a Bulgarian sphere of influence in some Slav State formations. The most important thing was that they created what was called by the Russian Academician Lihachov a 'state of the spirit', which would continue to live, even if the Bulgarian State were to fall into decline or even did not exist. The literature and historical works which were written were not limited within the framework of Bulgarian literature and requirements, but they had universal themes which incorporated Slav culture with the general European culture. It became the intermediary through which south and east Slav people became acquainted with the spiritual achievements of Christianity and Antiquity.

We mentioned the fact that the spread of Slavonic literacy took place through monks, who were missionaries spreading the Gospels among the Slav pagans. And here too we mention the fact that immediately after the Christianization of Bulgaria, the lights of many monasteries shone out over her territory. Thousands of monks in scores of scriptoria set to work to translate or multiply through copying from Greek into Bulgarian, not only the most necessary holy books for the divine service, but also the enormous philosophical heritage left by the Christian Church Fathers and works of literature (stories, narratives and hymns). The most gifted of them (Chernorisetz Hraber, Prezviter Cosma, Constantin Preslavski, Joan Exarh) wrote original works on various subjects and in various genres. And what had been preserved of ancient works in Byzantium also came onto the desks of the Bulgarian translators and copyists.

Ceramic icon of St Theodor Stratilat. 10th c. (white clay, drawn and with glaze)

THE DIRECTIONS AND THE TERRITORIES GAINED

The people nearest to the Bulgarians in the Balkans, the Serbs and Croatians, were the first to be subjected to this peculiar Bulgarian spiritual expansion. After the Bulgarians, the Serbs were the first to be converted to Christianity (879). But a little later their territory became part of Bulgaria in the ups-and-downs of the large-scale wars waged by the Bulgarian King Simeon the Great (893-927) against Byzantium. So it was that the invasion of the Old Bulgarian script and literature always took place within the framework of the Bulgarian State. Serbia would begin to live an independent State life again after the year 934, but the Slavonic script and literature would remain there.

It seems that the fate of the Slavonic script and literacy was much more complicated in the Croatian lands. The Bulgarian missionary would hand them on to thousands of Croatian converts to Christianity as early as the end of the ninth century. We have written 'it seems' because the divine service books which they brought and which became widespread in Croatia were in the Glagolitic alphabet, that is in the older of the two Slavonic alphabets (Glagolitic and Cyrillic). Later Catholicism would be established there with divine service and literacy in the Latin language. The Glagolitic

Enin Apostle, a Bulgarian Cyrillic-script monument of the mid-eleventh century

alphabet would, however, remain in Croatian literature as a symbol of the Croatian national spirit and national identity. This Glagolitic literacy would even flourish unexpectedly in the seventeenth and eighteenth centuries, after the Tridentine (the Council of Trent) at which the Papacy in reaction to the Reformation would allow the divine service in the native languages, although with some restrictions.

On their way towards the Slav lands in the south and the east of Europe, the Bulgarians would evangelize one non-Slav people too - the Rumanians. These descendants of the Dacians and of the Roman legions of the Emperor Trayan, who were left by Marcus Aurelius in 275 in the plains of Wallachia and Moldavia, were carefully and attentively persuaded by the Bulgarian missionaries to accept Christianity. The Rumanians would set up their own State only in the middle of the fourteenth century. The language of the Church, that is the Slavonic Bulgarian language, would become their official state language and this language would remain the same until the eighteenth century. Today it is obligatory for Rumanian historians to know the Old Bulgarian language to be able to read, analyse and research the public acts of former rulers and the literary works of their predecessors.

Piecemeal data bear witness to the fact that the Bulgarian missionary monks penetrated also among the Western Slavs, although in the long run they had no success there - Czechia and Poland remained in the zone of Catholicism and of the Latin language. In any case in 973 the Pope issued a bull against the 'unlawful

Church shroud. 18th c.

Bulgarian bishop in Prague'. But numerous sources bear witness to the fact that between 972 and 999 a Bulgarian bishopric was working in Krakow and that it had converted thousands of Slav pagans to Christianity.

But unquestionably the greatest success of the Bulgarians was in the enormous areas of Russia. 'The battle for Russia' would continue for nearly a century - officially the Russ would be converted to Christianity only in 988 and the way to this conversion was paved by hundreds of Bulgarian missionaries. They were broadcast like seeds in Russia from Murmansk on the Arctic Ocean to the mouth of the Dnieper on the Black Sea coast. Legend has it that the official conversion to Christianity took place according to the powerful command of the Russian King's wife, Olga, a princess of the Bulgarian royal court.

Father Dobreysho and John the Evangelist – a miniature in the Dobreysho Gospel

The spread of Christianity and of Slavonic literacy in Russia was of special significance for the expansion of her territory and the safeguarding of the Slavonic script and literature.

The expansion of Russia over one-sixth of the dry land of the earth from the seventeenth through the nineteenth century brought Christianity and literacy to all the Slavs and non-Slavs between Moscow and Vladivostok and between the Artic and China. To the West the Russians converted the Ukraine and Byelorussia to Christianity.

Of interest is the 'mutual preservation' of Slavonic literature achieved between the Bulgarian and Russian lands. In the period from the twelfth to the fourteenth century, Russia was invaded and dominated by the Tartars - almost all the cultural centres were

Cover of a Gospel, showing Climent of Ohrid. 14th c.

destroyed and burnt down. Just at that time Bulgaria was at the peak of her political power. Not only did she stop the Tartars' inroads into Europe but, just after the Battle of Kulikovo, she flooded the reinstated Russia with the rich literature of her scriptoria. The Russian historians call this activity 'the Second South Slav Influence' - of course, the first one was that in the ninth and tenth centuries. In the period from the fifteenth to the nineteenth century Bulgaria was subjugated to the Moslem Ottoman Empire and under its domination. It was already the time of the printed book, but the intolerance of Islamic fanaticism did not allow a single printing-house to work in the Bulgarian lands. Then wandering Russian monks flooded the Bulgarian churches and monasteries with books and other literary works and did not allow the Christian Word of God to die out.

WHAT
THE SLAVS READ
IN THE MIDDLE AGES

Let us begin with the written language. An all-Slav language no longer existed at about the time of the conversion of the Bulgarians to Christianity (the mid-ninth century). The national languages of the Russians, Poles, Czechs, Serbs and Croatians were well enough formed to exist as separate languages. But there were not any essential lexical and grammatical differences, so that the Old Bulgarian language was understandable enough. The fact that in the course of three hundred years no translation centres for Russian, Serbian and other languages were set up is somewhat puzzling. For instance, the Russians, Rumanians and Serbs copied the Bulgarian manuscripts literally 'photo-type' to the last comma. There were even some curious things - a famous collection of writings was copied in Russia for the Russian King Svetoslav in 1092, but on the title page there was a laudatory dedication to the Bulgarian King Simeon, who had ruled a century and a half before that. Obviously the original, from which they were copying, had been taken from the royal Bulgarian library. The

copiers had not dared to change one single line of the original, perhaps because of the canonicity of the Old Bulgarian alphabet and literature and because of the fear that any change might be considered heresy. In the twelfth century these fears seemed to have disappeared. In the fourteenth century, however, in the period of the 'Second Southern Slav Influence' there was a return to the Bulgarian originals. It lasted for a shorter period this time. So, what did the Slavs read in their own language? It was mostly translated literature. The Bible, of course, was in the first place. As is well known, it consists of fifty books of the Old Testament and twenty-seven books of the New Testament. They had been already translated as early as the middle of the ninth century, once by Methodius in Moravia (or in Byzantium for the Moravian Mission)

Old Bulgarian manuscripts

Page of the 'Six Days' by Joan Exarch, transcription of the 13th c.

The story of 'The Miracle Performed on the Bulgarian' - an Old Bulgarian work. 10th c.

'On the Letters' by Chernorizets Hraber, an Old Bulgarian work, end of 9th c.

and once by Presbyter Grigorius in the Bulgarian capital Preslav.

The Psalter held a special place. It was the most widespread work, obligatory for every Christian. This collection of poetical hymns was needed at any time of the day - reading a definite number of psalms was an obligatory part of the daily personal and social routine.

The Four Gospels - the basis of the Christian faith - also took up a considerable part of the literary output of the Slav writers. Along with the Four Gospels, dozens of apocryphal gospels, unacknowledged by the Church, were also in circulation.

The works of the priests - the Christian ideologists of Late Antiquity and the Middle Ages - were another part of the wealth of Slav literature.

In the field of secular literature they translated everything which could be found in Byzantium. It is well known that Byzantium preserved in its libraries and developed the ancient cultural traditions. Everything was translated into the Slav language. Slavdom became acquainted with the ancient cultural traditions long before West Europe. That is why the famous American medievalist Professor Ricardo Piccio may be right in insisting that it is more correct to speak of a Byzantine-Slav civilization than of Byzantine civilization.

And finally there are the original personal works - saints' lives, divine hymns, historical works, philosophical treatises and publicistic essays. Their genre and contents make them works of extraordinary literary value.

* * *

For many years Europe had only one patron acknowledged by canon law - Saint Benedict. In 1979 Pope John Paul II proclaimed the creators of the Slav alphabet, the Bulgarians Cyril and Methodius, to be also patrons of Europe. And this is the most important symbolical acknowledgment of the Bulgarian people's contribution to the development of European civilization.

7

С ЖЕ ... СТГО ЕVГЛІА ... С ... ПРОЖ

ство Хвѣмь, стыхъ отць. Га:

нига родетва Ï Хва. сна

двдка сна Авраамлıа. авра

амь роди Ісаака. Ісаакже

роди Іакова. Іаковъже роди

HISTORICAL SOURCES

TACITUS

Tacitus (55-117) was a Roman historian and author of 'Germania' which contains abundant information about the Old Germans.

I hesitate whether to deem the tribes of the Peutingers, Venetes and the Finns among the Germans or among the Sarmates, although the Peutingers, who are also called Bastarns, act like Germans... The Venetes have taken over most of their customs, because they wander about engaged in robbery in every part of the woods and mountains which are in the territories of the Peutingers and the Finns. It would be more correct to count them among the German tribes, because they build dwellings, carry shields and like to walk; all these things are different from the habits of the Sarmates, who live on carts and on horseback.

JORDANES - 'HISTORY OF THE GOTHS'

Setlements of Slavins, Anti and Bulgarians

Among these settlements is Dacia, protected on all sides by the towering Alps, encircling the land like a wreath. On the left side, to the north and at the source of the River Vistula, the numerous people of the Venetes live on a vast stretch of territory. It is true that the names of the Slavins, the Anti and the Bulgarians change in accordance with the tribes and places, but they are mostly called Slavins and Anti.

The Slavins inhabit the regions from Noviodunum (Isaktsa) and the so-called Lake Mursian (Balaton) as far as the Dniester and northward to the Vistula; moors and forests serve them as settlements. And the Anti, who are the bravest of them all, live from Danaster as far as Danaper (the Dnieper) where the Pontus

Euxinus makes a curve.

These rivers lie at a distance of many days journey apart. Beyond them, over the Pontus Euxinus, lay the territories inhabited by the Bulgarians, who became quite well-known because of the bad consequences of our sins.

PROCOPIUS

Procopius of Cesaree (circa 500-562) was the most prominent Byzantine historian of the sixth century.

The way of life of the Slavins and the Anti

These peoples - the Slavins and the Anti - are not ruled by one man. They have been living in democracy since ancient times and that is why they always discuss the useful and the difficult things together. It is almost the same with all other things with these two peoples and this has been known about these barbarians since time immemorial. And they think there is only one god, the creator of lightning. He is the one and only master of all. And they sacrifice oxen and all other kinds of animals to him. They do not know anything about Fate and they do not believe that it has any influence on man. And when they are faced by death, caused by illness or war, they promise that, if they survive, they will immediateley sacrifice what they have promised to their god for the sake of their souls. And after this they avoid the danger. They think that by means of this sacrifice , they have obtained redemption and are saved. Moreover, they worship rivers and nymphs and some other gods, and they offer sacrifices to all of them, and it is while they are making these offerings that they predict the future. Scattered about far from each other, all of them live in poor huts and change their settlements very often. When they engage in battle, most of them walk towards the enemy armed with small shields and spears; they do not put on chain armour. Some of them wear neither shirts nor even outer garments, but they fasten their loose trousers up to the privy parts and thus they battle with their enemies. The two peoples speak the same language - a completely barbarian one. Even in their outer appearance they do not differ from each other: all are tall and exclusively strong. Their bodies are not too white, nor is their hair very light blond, but they do not tend to be dark in colour and all are reddish. Like the Masagetes, they live a hard life and are completely negligent towards themselves and, like the Masagetes, they are also always covered with dirt. Still they are not evil or treacherous and even in their simplicity they keep to Hunnish ways and habits. What is more, the Slavins and the Anti used to bear the same name, because in ancient times both were called 'Spores', and I think it was beecause they used to live scattered all over their country. That is why they inhabit vast territories - the greatest part of the opposite bank of the River Danube. Well, that is more or less all there is to say about these people.

'THE HISTORY OF ARMENIA' BY MOSES OF HOREN

Moses of Horen (370-493) was one of the most prominent historians of ancient Armenia.

These lands (to the north of the Caucasus) were denuded of forests and then inhabited by settlers called Uhndur Bulgars (the Unogondur Bulgarians). Vund, one of their leaders gave his name to these lands which are called Vanand. Their settlements are called after the name of his (Vund's) brothers and descendants, even to the present day. In his day (that is in the time of the Armenian Tsar Artashes III, 422-428) there began a large-scale uprising in the ranges of the enormous Caucasus Mountains in the lands of the Bulgarians, many of whom, after they had broken away from Armenia, came to our land and settled for a long time in fruitful and fertile territory to the south of Coh (Colhida).

ENNODIUS -
'AN ECONOMIUM
OF KING THEODORIC'

Magnus Felix Ennodius (473-521) was born in France. He occupied a number of clerical posts. He was also in close relations with Theodoric, King of the Ostrogoths.

The chief of the Bulgarians is before my eyes, he was knocked down by your hand which defends freedom. He was not killed so as not to disasppear from history, but he was not left untouched so as not to be too bold in the future and to stay there among his undefeatable people - a living witness to your power. If he had been mortally wounded you would have beaten the man, but as he stayed alive he degraded his descent. The Bulgarians are a people who, before you came, had everything they wanted; they are a people who have acquired titles and gained their nobility in the blood of their enemies and for whom the battlefield glorifies the race, because they think without hesitation that the most noble is he whose weapon is covered with the most blood in the battle; they are a race of people who, before waging war against you, never chanced to face up to an opponent who would resist them, and they are a people who have waged wars with sudden attacks for a long time. They have never found it difficult, as one would have expected, crossing, as they do, the mountain ranges or the rivers in their way, or overcoming the lack of food because they think that drinking mare's milk is pleasure enough. Who could stand up to an enemy who rides on and feeds from his fleet-footed animal? And what would you say about the fact that they have even carefully taught these animals to adjust themselves to starving and exhaustion, and they can avoid hunger because of these mares. How does the rider obtain food from the udder of a hungry animal and how does he cleverly prevent the animal from hiding it? They used to believe that the world was open to them, now they think that only that part of the earth that you protect is out of their reach...

'A CHRONICLE' BY THEOPHANES THE CONFESSOR

The Founding of the Bulgarian State

In the years when Constantine (IV Pogonat) ruled in the West, Krobat (Kubrat), the ruler of the above-mentioned Bulgaria and of the Comrags, passed away. He left five sons. He had taught them to stand together at any price and to live together, so that they would rule over every land and never be slaves of another people. Shortly after his death his five sons separated and moved away from each other, each of them leading away that part of the people whom he had to rule over. And the first son, named Batbayan, kept to his father's behest and stayed on the land of his ancestors, his people living there through to the present day. But the second son, his brother, named Kotrag, crossed the River Tanais and settled opposite his elder brother. The fourth brother and the fifth crossed the River Ister, also called Danube. One of them remained with his army there in Avarian Patonia under the rule of the Hagan of the Avars, while the other one got to Pentanol in Ravenna (Italy) and submitted to the kingdom of the Christians. At last the third of them, called Asparuh, after he had crossed the Rivers Dnieper and Dniester, flowing to the north of the Danube, and after he had seized Oglos (north of the Danube), settled between the Danube and these rivers, because he saw that the place was naturally protected on all sides against any attack. There were fenlands in front of him and on all the other sides the place was encircled with rivers, like a garland. This ensured great security against the enemies of his people, who had been weakened by the separation. And after the Bulgarians had been separated in this way and had become less in number, there appeared the populous Hazar people from the innermost parts of Verzilia in the first Sarmatia and conquered all the lands beyond, as far as the Pontus Euxinus (the Black Sea). The first brother, Batbayan, the ruler of the first Bulgaria, became their vassal and he has been paying them taxes down to the present day. The Emperor Constantine who learned that an unwashed dirty people had unexpectedly settled in

Oglos, across the Danube, and had been attacking and devastating the lands near this river, the country which they already ruled and which had been ruled by the Christians before, became bitter and angry and ordered the armies to cross over into Thrace. After he had armed the fleet, he started out against them on land and sea, intending to drive them out with war. Sending the infantry in military order to attack them on land as far as the so-called Oglos and the Danube, he ordered the ships to anchor near the coast. The Bulgarians saw these numerous dense ranks and gave up all hope of saving themselves and fled into the fortifications, mentioned above, and got ready their defence. After they had not been daring enough to go out of the fortifications for three or four days and the Romans had not gone into battle against them because of the fens, the dirty people began to notice the shortcomings of the Roman fighters and screwed up their courage. Because the Emperor was suffering from pain in his foot and was forced to sail back to Mesembria with five ships and his attendants in order to take a water-cure, he left the strategists and the army with orders to skirmish with the Bulgarians to get them out of the fortifications and to go into battle against them. It happened, however, that they came out, for otherwise they would have been besieged and kept in their own fortifications. But the cavalrymen spread a rumour that the Emperor was running away. Then the Roman soldiers were seized with fear and they also spent their time running away, without anyone pursuing them. When the Bulgarians saw this, they began chasing them and killed most of them with their swords and wounded many of the others. They followed them as far as the Danube, crossed it and reached the so-called Varna, near Odessos, and the lands there. As they saw that the place was very seecure because the River Danube was behind and the ravines and the Pontus Euxinus covered their front line and sides, they decided, of all the Slav tribes, to settle the Severs in the lands from the front gorge up to Veregava (Rishki Pass), and the rest of the Seven Tribes, already paying them tribute, in the south and west territories as far as Avaria. And it came about that after they had extended their territories, they became vainglorius and began attacking and taking possession of the fortresses and the lands which were under the rule of the Romans. The Emperor was forced by the circumstances to conclude a peace treaty with them and agreed to pay them an annual tribute to the shame of the Romans, because of our numerous sins. It was surprising for the peoples both near and far to hear that the man who had made all of them pay tribute to him - peoples in the east and the west, in the north and the south - that he had been defeated by this dirty race of people who had just recently appeared. But he believed this had happened to the Christians according to God's providence and concluded a peace treaty, thinking in the way the Gospels taught. And he was not disturbed by his enemies to the end of his life.

AN ITALIAN LEGEND

An Italian legend, written by Father Gauderin in the tenth century.

1. In the time when the Emperor Michail ruled the Empire of the New Rome, there lived a man of noble birth, named Constantin, who had been born in the city of Thessaloniki. Called Philosopher, he deserved to be called so because his brillant intellect had been shining since the early years of his childhood. When he became a young man, he was taken to the capital by his parents. He was endowed with great piety and wisdom and, according to God's providence, he took holy orders and became a priest. In the meantime messengers of the Hazars had come to the Emperor, mentioned above, and begged him insistently to send them a learned and wise man who would really teach them the Catholic religion. Among other things, they added the following: "On the one hand the Jews and on the other hand the Saracens are trying to convert us to their religions. But we do not know which of them to choose and that is why we have decided to come for advice about our faith and salvation to you, the greatest Emperor of the universe, because we trust your loyalty and old freindship the most." Then the Emperor consulted the Patriarch and sent for the already mentioned Philosopher. After this, showing great respect for him, the Emperor sent him there with his messengers and the messengers of the Hazars, because he had complete trust in the man's wisdom and eloquence.

2. Once the necessary preparations had been made, Constantin started on his way and arrived in Herzon, which was situated very close to and neighbouring on

the lands of the Hazars. In this way he delayed his
arrival in order to learn the language of this people.

....

6. After these happenings the above-mentioned
Philosopher started on his way and came to the people
he had been sent to preach to, and he brought with him
the mercy of God, the Redeemer of All. All the people
who had been deceived by the slyness of the Saracens
and the Jews he freed from false beliefs by the power of
his eloquence. That was why the native people, who
were filled with joy, encouraged at being taught a true
religion, thanked the Almighty God and his minister
Constantin, the Philosopher.

They sent a letter to the Emperor, thanking him
that he had been so wholeheartedly zealous in bringing
them back into the true Catholic faith, and then
declared that was the reason they wished to be subordinate to his power and to be loyal to him forever. When
seeing the Philosopher off with great honour, they
offered him many presents but, like a true philosopher,
he refused to take any of them. Instead of giving him
presents, he asked them to set free all the Christians
they had captured, so that they could return with him.
They immediately did what he wished.

7. When the Philosipher returned to Constantino-
pole, the Moravian Prince Svetopolk heard about what
he had done in the lands of the Hazars. The Prince
cared a great deal about his people and send messengers to the above-mentioned Emperor and informed
him that his people had already given up paying
homage to idols and wished to keep to the Christan
law. But they had no one who could teach this law
perfectly and comprehensively. He asked the Emperor
to send such a man to his country, one who would
explain the beliefs and the requirements of the law, the
way to the truth to his people. The Emperor granted
him his request and asked the same above-mentioned
Philosopher to come to him, and he sent him with his
brother Methodius to the lands of the Slavs and
supplied them generously with money from his trea-
sury to cover their travelling expenses. God helped
them and they arrived in that country. The native
people heard of their forthcoming arrival and were
filled with joy, especially when they understood that
the brother carried the relics of Saint Climent and the
Scriptures, which had been translated into their own
language by the Philosopher. And so the people went
out of the city and met them and welcomed them, filled

with reverence and happiness. The Apostles eagerly began doing what they had come to do: they taught the children the alphabet, arranged divine service and used their eloquence like a sharp scythe to destroy the false beliefs which they found among the people. So after they had destroyed and rooted up the weeds of vice from the pernicious field, they sowed the seeds of God's Word. They stayed in Moravia for four and a half years, showed the way of the true faith to the people in this country and left there all the written works necessary for the divine service.

8. When His Holiness, Pope Nicolas, heard of all these things, he rejoiced exceedingly. He gave orders for papal letters to be sent to them, inviting them to visit him. When they received the message they also rejoiced and thanked the Lord God that they had been honoured and vouchsafed an invitation from the Papal Throne. They started at once and took some of their disciples with them, those who in their opinion were worthy to take holy orders. In a few days' time they arrived in Rome.

9. Because the above-mentioned Pope Nicolas had passed away not very long before, Adrian II succeeded him to the Papal Throne. And so he and the people showed their gratitude to the above-mentioned Philosopher for such a great blessing, they initiated his brother Methodius into episcopacy and some of the disciples into deaconship and priesthood.

10. When the same Philosopher named Constantin felt that the day of his death was near, with the permission of the Pope he renamed himself Cyril and said that he had had a divine revelation about it. So it came about that fifty days after this, on the sixteenth day before the March calends (February 14th) he passed on to God. The Pope ordered all the Greek and Roman clergymen to go to the funeral and sing psalms and religious songs, and burn incense and pay tribute to him in the way it was done only at the funeral of a Pope.

11. Then his brother Methodius, mentioned above, approached the Pope, knelt before him and said: "I consider it reasonable and honourable to tell Your Blessed Holiness, Our Papal Father, that when we started from our home on our mission, which God has helped us to fulfill, our mother begged us with tears in her eyes that if one of us died before we returned the brother who remained alive should take the dead one to his monastery and bury him there in a manner

proper and fittingg. So let Your Blessed Holiness vouch-safe and give the possibility to me, a most humble man, to fulfill my obligations, so that it may never seem that I have not fulfilled my mother's wish and what I swore to do." The Pope decided that he ought not to oppose such a petition and wish, although he found it some-what difficult. The corpse of the dead man had been carefully locked in a marble chest that had been sealed with the personal seal of the Pope. But then the Roman clergy, the bishops, the cardinals and the notable people in the city discussed the matter and went to the Pope, and began trying to persuade him to do what they wanted: "We consider it quite unworthy, Our Most Reverend Father and Bishop, that you should allow for some reason such an outstanding and glorius man to be taken away to another country. Our city and our Church received a treasure through his deeds and God showed him the way from far away foreign lands to our city and decided to take his soul to Heaven again from our city. And if you find it right, let him be buried here, because for a Christian it is the greatest honour to have a famous place for his burial in the most famous city in the world. The Pope liked the tenor of this advice and ordered the funeral to be in St. Peter's Church, that is to say in his own papal burial place.

12. When Methodius realised that his request had failed, he begged them again in the following words: "Since you have decided not to fulfill my request, I beg you importunately to let my brother be buried in the Chapel of the Blessed Climent, whose relics he brought here after he had worked so hard and with such great efforts to find them." The Holy Pontiff approved this request and, in the concourse of a big congregation of clerics and people and full of joy and deep reverence, they laid him in the tomb prepared for him, along with the marble chest in which the above-mentioned Pope had put him. This tomb is in the Chapel of the Blessed Climent, on the right side of the altar.

A SHORT LIFE
OF CLIMENT
BY DIMITER HOMATIAN

Dimiter Homatian was the Archbishop of Ohrid from 1216 to about 1234.

On this same day, June 27, in memory of our saintly Archbishop and miracle-working Climent, Bishop of Bulgaria in Ohrid.

1. This great priest and enlightener of Bulgaria was a native of European Moesia, the people of which are usually known to be Bulgarians.

2. First, along with godlike Naum, Angelari and Ghorasd, he zealously studied the Holy Bible, which had been translated by God's help into the local dialect by Cyril, a truly godly man and like the Apostles. From the beginning Climent had been with Methodius, the famous teacher of devotion to God and the Orthodox faith of the Moesian people.

4. In this way, obeying the divine laws from his youth and living righteously, exactly according to the Gospels, he finally became an adherent of the Christian leaders and the leader in Christian devotion of the whole Moesian people, bearing the same trials as the priests and the teachers - trials inflicted by the heretics, powerful in those days, as it is said in his lengthy, detailed Life.

5. Climent was raised to the bishop's throne when Methodius made him the bishop of the whole of Illia and of the Bulgarian people, who were predominant in the country. It was after the godly Cyril had moved and settled to a better life, and when he had made known his apostolic service and the growth of the talent with which he was gifted to Adrian, the then Pope of ancient Rome and when Methodius was made the archbishop of the whole of Moravia and Bulgaria by the same Pope.

6. Most often he stayed in the Illyrian city of Lichnida, which was the centre for the surrounding cities and which is today called Ohrid in the language of the Moesians, or in Cephalonia, translated into the Bulgaridn language Glavinitsa, where he left monuments.

7. In this city of Lichnida he built sacred temples and, starting with the very foundations, he erected a

holy monastery in the name of the martyr Pantelehmon, where he gave himself up to ascetic feats. As long as he lived he spread the rays of this teaching among his disciples, as though from a heavenly and lofty light. And when he moved into the joyful life among the Blessed, he left his sacred grave as a priceless treasure for his flock and as a possession worth as much as the whole world. Everyday this grave cured all kinds of diseases and, because of this, the holy monastery was given by God to be a common and gratuitous remedial hospice for all who were looking for help. But more about this later.

8. He left us these monuments and holy books in Ohrid - his own works, the works of his lofty mind and pen which are held in reverence and high honour by all the people, in the same way as are the written Word of God and the Tables of Moses.

9. There can be seen columns of stone in Cephalonia, preserved down to the present day. Inscriptions are carved on them and inform those who read them about the people who passed along and were converted to Christ.

10. Because the Bulgarian people were not yet fully enlighted, having only been christened and there was still barbarian wildness among them, he led everybody to the knowledge of God with his God-inspired precepts. Persuading the people to lead a righteous and just life, he turned the callousness of their mercy into nobility of character.

CHERNORIZETS HRABER.
ON THE LETTERS

Chernorizets Hrabar (The Brave) was an Old Bulgarian man of letters who was writing at the end of the ninth century and the beginning of the tenth century.

Then the Slavs had no books, and being pagans, they divined the future by lines and strokes. When they were christened they were forced to write the Slavonic language with Latin and Greek letters without their being adjusted. But how was it possible to write well in Greek letters: 'могъ' (I can) or 'жибот' (life), or 'ло', or 'цръку', or 'зъкъ', or 'гъ' or other similar words? And it went on so for many years.

After that God, the philanthropist, who arranges everything and does not leave mankind without native intelligence and salvation, took mercy on them. He sent Saint Constantin the Philosopher, named Cyril, who was a righteous and freedom - loving man and who thought up 38 letters, some of them on the model of the Greek letters and others in accordance with the Slavonic speech. First he began according to Greek: they said 'alpha', but he 'аз'(I). Both alphabeths begin with 'a'. And as the Greeks created their letters accordinng to the model of the Hebrew letters, he thought up the Bulgarian letters on the model of the Greek letters. The first letter in the Hebrew alphabet is 'aleph' which means 'learning'. When the child was first taken to school, they used to say to it: 'learn!' - this is 'aleph'. And the Greeks, imitating this, said 'alpha'. And they adjusted this Hebrew expression to the Greek. So they say to the child 'alpha' that in Greek means 'search', instead of 'Search for learning'. And, similar to this, Saint Cyril created 'Аз' (I). But it is the first letter and it has been given to the Slavs by God to loosen the mouths of those who teach themselves to reason by means of the alphabet, and that is why 'аз' is pronounced with a wide-open mouth, but the other letters with the mouth only slightly open.

These are the Slavonic letters and that is the way to write and pronounce them: А, Б В, right to Я and there are twenty-four of them. Similar to the Greek letters are the following ones: А, Б, Г, Д, Е, З, Н, (), К, Λ, М, Н, О, П, Р, С, Т, У, Ф, Х. Fourteen are according to the Slavonic language and they are the following: Б, Ж, Ц, Ш, Щ, Ъ, ЬІ, Ь, Ю.

Some say: "Why has he created 38 letters when it's possible to write with less - the Greeks write with 24 letters?" But these people do not know how many letters the Greeks write with. It is true the Greeks have 24 letters but they do not fill their books only with them. They have added 11 diphthongs and three for the numbers: 6, 30, 300. And their total is 38. Like this and in the same way Saint Cyril created 38 letters.

Other people say: "What is the use of Slavonic books?" They have not been created either by God or by angels, neither are they the original and fundamental ones like the Hebrew, Latin and Greek, which were the first and came from God."

Others think that God gave us our letters. And they do not know what they are talking about. They think that God has commanded all books to be written in three languages, as it is written in the Gospel: "There was a table (of laws) written down in Hebrew, Latin and Hellenic. But not in Slavonic. That is why the Slavonic books do not come from God."

But what can we say to such mad people? Let us give them our answer. As we have learned from the holy books everything comes, one thing after another, from God and not from anyone else. God did not create first of all either Hebrew or Hellenic, but Syrian which Adam spoke, and from Adam to the flood, and from the flood till God separated the languages when there was the babel, as it is written: "The languages got mixed up." And just as the languages got mixed up, so did the customs, regulations, laws and arts, according to the peoples. To the lot of the Egyptians fell the earthquake, while to the Persians, Chileans and Assyrians fell astrology, fortune-telling, wizardry and all the human arts. But to the Jews he gave the holy books in which it is written that God created the heaven, the earth and everything in it - man and everything he created in order, as it is written. And to the Hellenes he gave grammar, rhetoric and philosophy.

But before that the Hellenes had no letters for their own language and used Phoenician ones. And for many years it was so. But when Palamede came, he began from alpha and beta and invented letters for the Hellenes, but only 16. Cadum of Milin invented them too and added three more letters. They wrote with these 19 letters for a long time. Then Simonides invented and added two more letters and Epicharis, the writer, invented three more. And there were already 24 letters. Many years later Dionysus Grammaticus invented five, and someone else three for the numbers. And so for many years a great number of people were hardly able to get together 38 letters. After many years had passed, at God's bidding they found seventy men to translate the Holy Writ from Hebrew into the Greek language. But Saint Constantin, called Cyril, translated the Slavonic books alone and he created the letters in a few years. It had taken those many people - seven persons - a great number of years to create the alphabet and seventy people had done the translation of the Bible. That is why the Slavonic letters are more sacred and they deserve more reverence, because they were created by a saintly man but the Greek letters were created by pagan Hellenes.

But if anybody were to say that he had not adapted the letters well and that they were still being adapted, we would give this answer. In the same way Achilla and Symaches adapted the Greek letters many times and other people did the same after them. Because it is easier to adapt than to invent them for the first time.

If you were to ask the Greek men of letters: "Who created your letters or who translated your books or when was that?", you would see that it is seldom that anyone of them knows. But if you asked a Slav child, who is learning it's ABC: "Who created your alphabet?" or "Who translated your books," all of them would know and they would answer "Saint Constantin the Philosopher, called Cyril: he and his brother Methodius created the alphabet and translated the books." And if you were to ask when it was, they would know and would say that it was in the lifetime of the Greek King Michael, of the Bulgarian King Boris, of the Moravian Prince Rastitsa and of the Blatenian Prince Cotsel, and they would say that it was in the year 6363 of the creation of the world (855).

There are other answers, but we will give them in other places because now there is no time. So, brethen, God has given to the Slav reason. Glory and honour to Him, power and worship to Him, now and forever in the endless centuries, Amen.

MARGINALIA AND POSTSCRIPTS

The postcripts to the Old Bulgarian translation of the Life of Antonius the Great, written at the end of the ninth century and the beginning of the tenth

by Joan, the unworthy presbyter who did this translation.But as for me, the sinner, as I finish the translation of the work by Atanasius the Great on the life of Our Great Father Antonius, I would like to have a little talk with all the monks who are listening to me and, in general, with ordinary believers. And I beg you to forgive me if we have put some word wrong or have used it clumsily in translating his miracles. Because we are not so experienced in rendering those words from the Hellenic which are missing in the Slavonic language, and so we have tried to convey their meaning. And we did not rely only on our own minds, but were

helped on by the worthy servant of God, Joan, who
followed Antonius's Life. We were requested to translate by the church builder Joan, our master, Archbishop of the Bulgarian lands. And we were asked to
translate not only the Life of Antonius but also the Life
of the famous miracle-working disciple of Peter,
Pancratius, because it had not been translated by
anyone before us. When I thought it out, I decided to
overcome our crudeness and inexperience and not to
leave the Slav people deprived of the divine 'Lives' of
these miracle-workers. And I understood that the lay
brothers would not be deprived of the award of great-
ness of soul, given by our Lord God and Saviour, Jesus
Christ, when he has to present to God the pure souls of
the people. Glory to them and to the Father and Son
and the Holy Ghost, now and forever and through the
eternal centuries.

*

Grigorius, the Presbyter's marginalia to the translation of the Old Testament (end of the ninth century and beginning of tenth)

Books of the holy Old Testament which reveal
characters found in the New Testament and the truth.
They have been translated from the Greek into the
Slavonic language in the time of the Royal Prince
Simeon, the son of Boris, by Grigorius, the Presbyter,
churchman of all the Bulgarian churches. These books
have been translated by order of the princely book-
lover Simeon, quite rightly called lover of God.

*

Marginalia to the translation of "Words against the Arians" by Atanasius of Alexandria (907)

Jesus Christ, Son of God, be victorious!

These devout books, called Atanasius, have been
translated by the orders of our Bulgarian Prince Simeon
from the Greek language into Slavonic by the Bishop
Constantin, who was a disciple of Methodius, the

Moravian Archbishop, in the year 6414 (906) from the beginning of the world. And they were written at the same Prince Toudor's orders by the monk Black Shirt Doscov at the mouth of the River Ticha, where the same Prince Toudor built a beautiful, holy, new, gold church in the year 6415 (907) indict 14. In the same year, on the second day of May, Saturday evening, the father of this Prince died - God's servant, our high-minded and pious Bulgarian Prince, called Boris, whose Christian name was Michael. He lived purely, professing the Orthodox faith in our Lord Jesus Christ. This Boris converted the Bulgarians to Christianity in the year 6374 (864). In the name of the Father, the Son and the Holy Ghost, Amen.

*

Saint George's miracle performed on the Bulgarian in the tenth century

Once there came a wandering brother. He carried a Cross with which he performed many miracles. And after he had stayed here for several days, he fell ill and called me. And when I went to him in the inn where he was lying, he said to me: "Bless me, Father, and pray to God for me! Take this Cross! The story of it is long, but I have no strenght to tell you about it. I see the end of my life has come, but if God should help me, I will tell you a little about it. Then I called the abbot and three old men (Friars) and after we had prayed for him, he raised himself from his couch, sat down, crossed himself and told us the following:

"Father Abbot Peter! I am one of the newly-christened Bulgarian people, whom God enlightened in these years with holy christening through his representative Prince Boris, called Michael in his sacred christening. With the power of Christ and with the sign of the Cross he won over the hard-hearted and refractory Bulgarian tribe and with the light of reason he enlightened the heart of this tribe, troubled by the ill-meaning deeds of the Devil. He brought the people back from the Devil's dark, deceptive, stinking victims, abhorrent to God, brought the tribe out of darkness into light, from deception and wrong-doing to the truth; did away with the Bulgarians' foul-smelling and dirty foods, knocked down their sacrificial altars, strengthened their positions with holy books on the Orthodox Christian faith, and brought the Archbishop, Saint Joseph (Stephan), and other teachers and mentors to them, and built churches and monasteries, appointed bishops, priests and abbots, and all of them had to lead his people along God's holy way. Then God honoured him and he assumed the image of an Angel. Departing from this life of deception, he presented himself to Jesus Christ in the Jerusalem on high.

"But while he was still alive in retirement in a monastery and Vladimir, his eldest son, ruled in his place with God's blessing and Michael's blessing, Simeon dethroned his brother and ascended the throne. Then the Magyar people rose against him and his people were led into captivity - he fought against the Magyars but they defeated him. I also took part in this war in that year. I had not any rank then and did not live where the Prince lived, but outside with the people. When the Magyars drove us away, my horse became dead tired and I found myself running with fifty men along the path and the Magyars were pursuing us. And I shouted in a loud voice: 'Lord God of the Christians! Help me through the prayers of the great martyr George and save me.' And then I turned in prayer to Saint George and said: 'Saint George, in the holy christening you gave me your name; I am your servant, now save me from the pagans.' Then the right front leg of my horse stumbled and sank into the ground and broke, and the people in my battalion ran away from me. Nearby were a forest and a valley. I bent my bow and with arrows in my hand got down from my horse. And when I looked round and saw the Magyars running towards my horse, I shouted: 'Lord God, Jesus Christ, have mercy on me and send your pious servant and martyr George to protect and save me in this hour.' As soon as I said these words weeping, my horse came to me with its leg whole and the Magyars were running after it: they wanted to catch it, but none of them could get near it. And I said again: 'Glory to you, O Lord, because you are not far from those who call you with all their hearts. Great George, be with me.' Then I got onto my horse and, although the Magyars were after me and shot many arrows at me, they did not hurt me because of the strength of God and the help of Saint George. And immediately I found myself in my village, which was three days' distance from the place where the Magyars had shot at me. There were only two people of my battalion who came back, and it was on the second day after my return. All the others had been overtaken by the enemy and killed.

"After that, when Simeon heard that the Magyars would come again, he led us once more to war. And while I was lying at home with my wife, a beardless man appeared in front of me. Such a bright light shone from him that I could not look into his face. He said to me: 'George, you have to go to war, but buy yourself another horse, because the one that you have now will die unexpectedly on the third day after it sets out with you. And then I order you to skin its leg, the one which was fractured, and to see how great is the power of the Most Holy Trinity and how great is the help of the holy martyr George. Do not use what you will find on this leg for anything except for the honour of the Cross and do not speak about it until you see the glory of God.' And I asked: 'Sir, who are you whose face I cannot look into?' - 'I am,' he answered, 'George, the servant of Christ, whom you, the man who prayed, called to for help.' And when I got up from sleep, I glorified God and Saint George and, after that, I bought another horse, just as the saintly man had ordered me to do. Before I went to the war, I called the priest to hold a divine service, I killed my most valuable ox, slaugthered ten sheep and ten pigs, and gave everything to the poor. And I went to war with two horses. On the third day of my journey there, the first horse became ill, fell down and died. The battalion did not want to let me skin its leg because we were in a hurry, but when I told them how it had fractured its leg while we were galloping, they waited for me. So we skinned the leg and found, under the knee, three iron splints, which held the bone firmly, and the bone was not broken, but only cracked length-wise. We tried very hard to take off the iron splints, but we did not succed. Then we cut off the bone, put it on a stone and broke it into pieces with our axes, and it was only then that we were able to take off the splints. After that we wondered at the great and incredidle power of the Holy Trinity and at the ready help of the saintly martyr George. We glorified God and went to the war. And by the mercy of God nobody died in this war and we all got back safe and sound.

"When we came back home, I found my wife ill with a fiery hot fever. After I had been there for a week or two and saw that she was suffering very much, I plucked up my courage and ventured to pray: 'O God, through the prayers of the woman who bore Thee and of the saintly George, cure your servant Maria!' Then

I put three of the iron splints on her body and she recovered and glorified God and the great martyr George. And when I understood the mercy and the goodness of the Holy Trinity, I called the farrier and said to him: 'Brother, forge a Cross for me out of these iron splints.' He made the Cross for me, just as the saintly man had told me to have it made.

"And there have been many other miracles performed with this Cross; mad furies have been cast out of the people with it and they have saved themselves from disasters and wars with the prayers of the Saint and Martyr, George."

Bojidar Dimitrov
BULGARIANS – CIVILIZERS OF THE SLAVS

Editor of the Bulgarian Text: Vyara Kandjeva
English Translation: Marjorie Hall Pojarlieva
Photographers: Vyara Kandjeva, Dimiter Angelov, Antoniy Handjiysky

Publishing House BORINA
P.O.Box 105; 1408 Sofia
Bulgaria

ISBN 954 500 033 3

Printed by Publishing Co K & M, Bulgaria